AGING EASY
A Resource Guide

Dr. Mondresia Carver

AGING EASY: A Resource Guide

ISBN: 978-1-7363032-9-0

AGING EASY: A Resource Guide

Table of Contents

AGING EASY: A Resource Guide

INTRODUCTION

People often ask, "Why Seniors?" My response is always the same, "Why NOT Seniors?" I have always had an unwavering desire to serve and protect the elderly. Even as a child, when given the opportunity to choose, my choice was always to be in the company of the "older folk". I have found their wisdom and conversation to be priceless.

For Seniors, living independently during their golden years can be an enjoyable and rewarding time of life. Most desire to maintain their dignity, quality of life, and independence while living at home. Sounds simple enough. However, what I have found to be true, both professionally and personally, is that things aren't always so simple.

As a very young adult, I can recall experiencing the loss of my maternal great-grandmother. Having not been afforded the knowledge that I currently possess, watching her cognitive decline over a 5-year span was painful. On the day of her funeral, I can still recall feeling as though I'd lost my grandmother several years prior. A better understanding of her diagnosis would have added more quality to the time we shared. Experiencing the loss of my paternal grandmother was another taxing experience. Though her diagnosis did not rob her of her cognitive ability, Cancer certainly took everything else. During this experience, my knowledge base for the situation was greater. Therefore, medical attention, placement, and long-term planning were much easier. Most recently, the loss of my maternal grandfather was a challenge that tugged on every ounce of knowledge, experience, and emotion possible. Within a 7-month period, I watched my grandfather drift from what most called, "The World's Oldest Teenager" to being completely bedridden and dependent on others for care. Heart attack, stroke, cancer, kidney failure, dialysis, feeding tube, tracheostomy, cardiac arrest, and resuscitation were only among the most significant challenges that he endured. Fortunately, my family and I were able to make "informed" decisions to assure that he maintained quality of life.

Working in Senior care for over 20 years, I have been exposed to all aspects. I have consoled weeping widows. I have found placement for seniors who have no family. I have advocated for seniors who were mistreated by family and/or professionals. I have found assistance for seniors that wanted to remain at home but needed a little help. I have helped family to understand that Hospice is actually very beneficial and not death sentence. I have hired good caregivers. I have terminated poor caregivers. I have also provided Psychotherapy for seniors who suffer from depression and anxiety. In short, Seniors and their families experience the same issues as those in other populations. For me, it is a God-given charge that I do all that is within my power to assure that this population is provided with the supports needed to be safe, healthy, and happy.

What's Affected?	What Helps?
Cardiovascular System	• Include physical activity in your daily routine. • Eat a healthy diet. • Don't smoke. • Manage stress. • Get enough sleep.
Bones/joints/muscles	• Get adequate amounts of calcium. • Get adequate amounts of vitamin D. • Include physical activity in your daily routine. • Avoid smoking and limit alcoholic drinks.
Digestive system	• Eat a healthy diet. Drink plenty of water and other fluids. • Include physical activity in your daily routine. • Don't ignore the urge to have a bowel movement.
Bladder/urinary tract	• Go to the toilet regularly. • Maintain a healthy weight. • Don't smoke. • Do Kegel exercises. • Avoid Caffeine, acidic foods, alcohol, and carbonated beverages. • Eat more fiber.
Memory/ thinking skills	• Include physical activity in your daily routine. • Eat a healthy diet. • Stay mentally active. • Be social. • Treat cardiovascular disease. • Quit smoking.
Eyes/Ears	• Schedule regular checkups. • Follow your doctor's advice about glasses, contact lenses, hearing aids and other corrective devices. • Wear sunglasses or a wide-brimmed hat when you're outdoors and use earplugs when you're around loud machinery or other loud noises.
Teeth	• Brush and floss regularly. • Visit your dentist or dental hygienist for regular dental checkups.
Skin	• Bathe or shower in warm — not hot — water. Use mild soap and moisturizer. • When you're outdoors, use sunscreen and wear protective clothing. • Don't smoke.
Weight	• Include physical activity in your daily routine. • Eat a healthy diet. • Watch your portion sizes.
Sexuality	• Share your needs and concerns with your partner.
	• Get regular exercise. • Your doctor might offer specific treatment suggestions.

THE SILVER YEARS

What does aging look like?

Aging has been noted to causes changes in the biological, physiological, environmental, psychological, behavioral, and social processes. Some of these changes are benign, such as graying hair. Others cause functional declines to include the functioning of the senses, activities of daily life, increased susceptibility to and frequency of disease, frailty, and disability. In fact, much of the aging process contributes to major risk factors for a number of chronic diseases in humans. Research is ongoing to identify the interactions among genetic, environmental, lifestyle, behavioral, and social factors and their influence on the initiation and progression of age-related diseases and degenerative conditions.

We all know that aging will cause wrinkles and gray hair. But did you know that aging will affect your teeth, heart and sexuality? As things become less perky and dependable, close attention should be given to your cardiovascular system, bones/joints/muscles, digestive system, bladder/urinary tract, memory/ thinking skills, eyes, ears, teeth, skin, and weight.

I JUST FORGOT TO REMEMBER

What is Dementia?

According to the National Institute on Aging, "Alzheimer's disease is an irreversible, progressive brain disorder that slowly destroys memory and thinking skills and, eventually, the ability to carry out the simplest tasks. It is the most common cause of dementia in older adults. While dementia is more common as people grow older, it is not a normal part of aging."

Dementia is the loss of cognitive functioning—thinking, remembering, and reasoning—and behavioral abilities to such an extent that it interferes with a person's daily life and activities. These functions include memory, language skills, visual perception, problem solving, self-management, and the ability to focus and pay attention. Some people with dementia cannot control their emotions, and their personalities may change. Dementia ranges in severity from the mildest stage, when it is just beginning to affect a person's functioning, to the most severe stage, when the person must depend completely on others for basic activities of living. While dementia is more common as people grow older (up to half of all people age 85 or older may have some form of dementia), it is not a normal part of aging. Many people live into their 90s and beyond without any signs of dementia.

Signs and symptoms of dementia result when once-healthy neurons (nerve cells) in the brain stop working, lose connections with other brain cells, and die. While everyone loses some neurons as they age, people with dementia experience far greater loss. Dementia symptoms vary depending on the cause, but common signs and symptoms include:

Cognitive changes

- Memory loss, which is usually noticed by a spouse or someone else
- Difficulty communicating or finding words
- Difficulty with visual and spatial abilities, such as getting lost while driving
- Difficulty reasoning or problem-solving
- Difficulty handling complex tasks
- Difficulty with planning and organizing
- Difficulty with coordination and motor functions
- Confusion and disorientation

Psychological changes

- Personality changes
- Depression
- Anxiety
- Inappropriate behavior
- Paranoia
- Agitation
- Hallucinations

It is important to note that, certain medical conditions can cause serious memory problems that resemble dementia. These problems should go away once the conditions are treated. These conditions include:

- Side effects of certain medicines

- Emotional problems, such as stress, anxiety, or depression
- Certain vitamin deficiencies
- Drinking too much alcohol
- Blood clots, tumors, or infections in the brain
- Delirium
- Head injury, such as a concussion from a fall or accident
- Thyroid, kidney, or liver problems

Caring for a person with Alzheimer's or dementia often involves a team of people.

Ways to Cope

- Talk openly about the changes you are experiencing.
- Identify any emotional needs. Meet with a counselor specializing in treating families dealing with a chronic illness.
- Don't pull away. Try to find activities you can still enjoy together.
- Make it OK to laugh. Sometimes humor lightens the mood and makes coping easier.
- Record thoughts, feelings and wisdom in writing, audio, or video.
- Establish a plan of care. Organize documents you may need into a file.
- Research/Identify available resources.
- Discuss any role changes in the relationships.
- Connect with others experiencing a similar situation.

IT'S ON THE REFRIDGERATOR

Where's all the information when you need it?

Caregiving can slowly become a reality as a loved one ages, or it can be a sudden change resulting from an accident, a new diagnosis, or a hospitalization. Regardless of your individual situation, it is crucial to understand that the nature of providing care for someone can change in an instant. For this reason, it is especially important to approach caregiving in an organized fashion. Should anything change, you will have a plan of action to build off and a list of available resources ready to help you meet new and emerging needs. Proactive planning increases the likelihood that a loved one will be able to afford the lifestyle they have in mind for the future, guarantees that their health care and end-of-life wishes are respected even if they can't convey them, and clearly specifies how their estate will be administered. Your loved one's participation in setting these goals is paramount, so long as they are still competent to make these decisions.

Step 1: Gather information and address any problem(s) at hand.
Step 2: Review your loved one's home environment, activities of daily living (ADLs), health status, medical and legal documents, and financial situation to ensure nothing is overlooked.
Step 3: Identify Care Needs
Step 4: Set Goals of Care

Step 5: Identify who is responsible for assisting with each goal.
Step 6: Review/Modify/Update as needed.

SOMEONE CALL 911!

What information do I need for a hospital visit?

The dreadful call advising that your loved one is being transported to the hospital can be traumatizing all in itself. The admission of elderly patients to hospital, their treatment and subsequent discharge can prove challenging. If you are prepared as the previous chapter advised, the hospital admission should be less problematic.

Tips for Hospitalizations:

1. Establish open communication with the hospital staff.
   Identify your loved one's primary hospital doctor and the names of any specialists on their care team.

2. The primary physician is in charge of coordinating your loved one's care and the staff members providing it. The case manager, charge nurse or nurse manager should be able to give you this information.

3. Determine how your loved one will pay for their care.
   A good place to start is determining whether the senior has Medicare, Medicaid, or private insurance.

4. The hospital social worker is your greatest asset when it comes to figuring out what insurance your loved one has, how much

it will cover and what other programs might be available to help offset the costs of care both inside and outside the hospital.

5. Learn about post-hospitalization care, medication and equipment needs. Prescription medications may be added to a senior's daily regimen. Inpatient or outpatient physical therapy, occupational therapy and/or speech language pathology may be necessary. Durable medical equipment and other devices might be needed to enhance their mobility and functioning.

6. Decide where the senior should live during/after they recovery.
   Part of understanding your loved one's health status and care needs directly influences the setting in which these needs can be met.
   The level of care they require will determine where they will be discharged to.
   Many seniors need high-level skilled nursing care in a rehabilitation facility to regain partial or total functioning before they can return to their home or even move in with a caregiver.
   Perhaps it is no longer safe for the senior to live at home, in which case they will need to move to a skilled nursing facility, an assisted living facility or set up extensive help through an in-home care

company.

7. Make sure all important legal documents are in order.
   There are several crucial legal documents that all adults should have in place. Medical and financial powers of attorney, advance directives, HIPAA authorization and estate planning documents (such as a will) are typically central pieces of the legal puzzle for seniors and their caregivers.

8. Educate yourself on the senior's medical condition.
   Learn all you can about their medical condition(s) and the medications they are taking. A solid understanding of their health is invaluable and makes you a strong and effective member of their care team.

9. Get support for yourself.
   Contact your local Area Agency on Aging to find out what resources are available.

Hospital Discharge

A significant proportion of patients who experience delayed discharge are elderly. Poor hospital bed management and a failure of communication between health and social care are the principal contributing factors. Effective discharge planning includes:

- Involvement of the patient and their family in decisions about their care.
- Hospital multidisciplinary teams associated with acute admission facilities working in an integrated manner.
- Adequate and timely transfer of information between services.
- Timely provision of discharge and support packages.
- Adequate information to patients and families about financial and social supports.

I'M GOING HOME!

What supports are available for at-home living?

According to the American Psychological Association, 61% of Americans over the age of 65 reported that they would prefer to live in their own home as they age. Though living alone can give seniors more independence and freedom, it comes with safety risks such as misuse of medication, malnutrition, injury, and more. If your loved one has opted to live alone, here are a few safety tips:

1. Remove Tripping Hazards

To help minimize the danger of falls for seniors, make sure all loose objects have been removed from walking areas to include shoes, magazines, boxes, and blankets. Remove any open extension cords that could present a falling hazard.

2. Keep the Home Well-Lit

Lack of sufficient lighting can increase the risk of danger for seniors who live alone. Keeping staircases, hallways, and pathways properly lit can help prevent falls. Consider installing nightlights or wireless motion sensor lights throughout the home.

3. Minimize Slippery Surfaces

Remove rugs or secure them with a non-slip backing. Install carpeting or non-slip rubber treads on any hardwood staircases to prevent slipping.

4. Safety Railings
Bathroom modifications for elderly can include installing grab bars inside the tub/shower area and next to the toilet. Assure sturdy railings on both sides of all staircases.

5. Fire Safety
Put a smoke detector and fire extinguisher on every floor of the home and test them regularly. All doors and windows should open easily from inside. Be sure to develop an escape plan.

6. Prescriptions
Go over prescription safety information with your senior, including drug and food interactions. Pill organizers are helpful. Maintain a record of all the medications your senior is taking.

7. No Dangerous Housework
Never let your senior undertake dangerous work around the house. While your loved one may insist that he or she is capable of changing an overhead bulb or moving a piece of furniture, these activities can be extremely dangerous. If there is a job that requires getting up on a stepladder or lifting heavy objects, either do it for your senior or hire someone else to do it.

8. Stock the Pantry
To prevent malnutrition, keep the fridge and pantry well stocked with nutritious food. Make sure your senior is able to buy groceries or set up a service to take care of the grocery shopping each week. Remember to keep items in cabinets

low enough that they can be reached easily.

THEY SAID I CAN'T GO HOME!

What supports are available when returning home is no longer an option?

At some point, support from family, friends, and local programs may not be enough to provide sufficient care for your senior. This responsibility may even become overly taxing to the caregiver. Seniors who require 24-hour assistance might find that a moving to a residential facility that provides long-term care services is a better option.

Facility-based long-term care services include: board and care homes, assisted living facilities, nursing homes, and continuing care retirement communities.

Some facilities offer only housing and housekeeping, some include personal care and medical services. Many facilities offer special programs for people with "Alzheimer's disease and other types of dementia."

Placement Type	Description	Estimated Price Range
Board Homes/ Personal Care Homes	Board and care homes, also called residential care facilities or group homes, are small private facilities, usually with 20 or fewer residents. Rooms may be private or shared. Residents receive personal care and meals and have staff available around the clock. Nursing and medical care usually are not provided on site.	$1800 per month & up
Assisted Living/Independent Living	Assisted living is for people who need help with daily care, but not as much help as a nursing home provides. Assisted living facilities range in size from as few as 25 residents to 120 or more. Typically, a few "levels of care" are offered, with residents paying more for higher levels of care. Assisted living residents usually live in their own apartments or rooms and share common areas. They have access to many services, including up to three meals a day; assistance with personal care; help with medications, housekeeping, and laundry; 24-hour supervision, security, and on-site staff; and social and recreational activities. Exact arrangements vary from state to state.	$2300 per month & up
Skilled Nursing Facilities	Nursing homes, also called skilled nursing facilities, provide a wide range of health and personal care services. These services typically include nursing care, 24-hour supervision, three meals a day, and assistance with everyday activities. Rehabilitation services, such as physical, occupational, and speech therapy, are also available. Some people stay at a nursing home for a short time after being in the hospital. After they recover, they go home. However, most nursing home residents live there permanently because they have ongoing physical or mental conditions that require constant care and supervision.	$5000 per month & up
Continuing Care Retirement Community	Continuing care retirement communities (CCRCs), also called life care communities, offer different levels of service in one location. Many of them offer independent housing (houses or apartments), assisted living, and skilled nursing care all on one campus. Healthcare services and recreation programs are also provided.	$2200 per month & up

HELP, I CAN'T DRIVE ANYMORE

What are some options for transportation?

With failing health and change on care needs comes the constant need for assistance that had not previously been considered. What happens when there's a doctor's appointment and your senior is no longer able to drive? What happens when you've got a meeting and your senior has a doctor's appointment at the same time? These are questions and concerns that most individuals in your situation have. Be assured, there are options.

Medical/Nonmedical Transportation: Uber is the best-known taxi alternative. Uber connects passengers to drivers via smartphone in countries around the world. Payments are made through an app, avoiding the need to carry cash. Rates vary but can be a good deal. For example, a taxi from my office to a nearby college campus would cost $37. The same trip with Uber would cost $16 to $51, depending upon the type of car I select.

That $16 fare looks like a steal. However, Uber adjusts its fares in real time based on traffic, demand, and weather, and some riders who've been hit with high "surge fares" have complained. Stories of Uber riders charging $300 or more for short trips have made the news since at least 2013. Veteran Uber users recommend you avoid surprises by always getting a fare estimate before you book your ride. Lyft is another ridesharing service available in many US cities. The taxi ride that would cost

$16 with Uber and $37 with a local cab company will cost $26 or $39 with Lyft, depending on the service level. Lyft has a pricing policy similar to Uber's, with "prime time" fares up to twice as high as regular rates, so again, it pays to get an estimate before booking.

Public Transportation: Most public transit authorities offer special transportation services for seniors and riders who can't use regular bus and rail lines. For example, the Metro Access program in Austin, Texas, provides shared rides along existing service routes for riders with mobility issues, and the Access-A-Ride program offers deeply discounted on-demand taxi service. A Metro Access monthly pass costs less than $50.
Riders who don't qualify for special access can call a cab to get to and from doctor appointments and to the grocery store. Most services will quote you a fare in advance over the phone or online — no app needed.

Home Care Agencies: Home Care/Private Duty Caregivers often include errand and appointment transportation in their services, sometimes for an additional fee. Rates vary by region; the average US home health aide cost is about $20 per hour.

Family members/Friends: Caring for our senior takes a village. Schedule a meeting with family members and friends to discuss how they might be able to assist.

If these options aren't available where you live or if the cost is too high, check with your area senior center and with local service organizations to see if there are any volunteer programs offering rides for seniors. Giving up driving isn't something any of us look forward to but going carless doesn't have to mean being stranded at home.

WHO'S PAYING FOR THIS?

Who is responsible for what?

There are various ways of paying for senior housing and long-term care; some of the most frequently accessed sources are summarized here.

- Private Funds
- Senior Living Line of Credit
- Medicaid
- Medicare
- Long-Term Care Insurance
- Supplemental Security Income (SSI)
- Veteran's Benefits – Aid and Attendance
- Life Settlements

Medicaid versus Medicare

What is Medicaid?	As defined in Title XIX of the Social Security Act, Medicaid is a joint Federal-State program which pays for medical services to eligible needy and vulnerable families and individuals. The State must offer basic services in order to receive Federal matching funds, and the Medicaid program varies from State to State. Medicaid is intended to pay for health and long-term care for persons with limited financial resources.
What does Medicaid cover?	Outpatient hospital services Inpatient hospital services Nursing facility services for persons aged 21 or older. Prenatal care Physician services Medical and surgical dental services Home health and community-based care for persons eligible for nursing facility services Laboratory and x-ray services Nurse-midwife services Pediatric and family nurse practitioner services Family planning services and supplies
Payment for Medicaid Services	Medicaid is a vendor payment program, and States may pay for Medicaid services through HMOs or directly to providers. The Medicaid payment rates must be accepted as full payment in full. States may elect to impose deductibles, coinsurance, or co-payments on Medicaid recipients for some services.
Medicaid & Nursing Home Care	Medicaid currently pays for 60% of nursing facility care.
Medicaid and Assisted Living / Home and Community-Based Services	Medicaid pays for only about 10 percent of assisted living services, the majority being paid for with private funds. Several states have adopted Medicaid waiver programs to earmark funds towards assisted living, and this trend is expected to continue as cost containment remains a critical issue for both State and Federal governments.

What is Medicare?	Provided automatically to individuals 65 and over who are entitled to Social Security, and to disabled persons who have received such benefits for at least 24 months. As defined in Title XVIII of the Social Security Act, Medicare ("Health Insurance for the Aged and Disabled") is a Federal health insurance program for aged (65+) and certain disabled individuals (e.g., persons with end-stage renal disease (ESRD) who require dialysis or a kidney transplant), regardless of income.
Part A	Provided to almost all U.S. residents 65 or older, certain aliens 65 or over, and disabled individuals entitled to Part A.
Part B	Supplemental Insurance. Part B coverage requires payment of a monthly premium, and primarily covers physician services. Also covered by Part B are non-physician services, including diagnostic tests, ambulance services, clinical laboratory tests, flu vaccinations, and some therapy services.
Skilled Nursing Coverage	Covered by Part A only if it follows within 30 days of a hospitalization of three or more days and is certified as medically necessary. Medicare does generally not pay for long-term care in a nursing facility, and the number of SNF days provided for is limited to 100 days, with a co-payment required for days 21 to 100.
Home Health Agency Coverage	Can be furnished by a home health agency at the residence of the beneficiary. Part A may also pay for some medical equipment and medical supplies.
Inpatient Hospital Coverage	Includes coverage of the costs for most hospital services, including operating room, intensive care, laboratory tests, inpatient prescription drugs, X-rays, rehabilitation, long-term hospitalization, meals, and semi-private room.

CALL MY ATTORNEY!

When is legal advisement needed?

Long-term objectives like financial planning, advance care planning, estate planning and funeral planning should be addressed sooner than later. Planning is most effective when you or your loved one is cognitively able to participate in the decision making. These preparations are extremely important and can be time sensitive, depending on your loved one's current situation.
For more complex medical, legal, and financial aspects of a care plan are best handled by experienced elder care experts. Specialists, such as elder law attorneys, therapists, benefits counselors, certified public accountants (CPAs), financial advisors, geriatricians, and social workers, can be valuable additions to an elder's care team. If your caregiving situation is particularly complex, a reputable geriatric care manager can assist in organizing, monitoring, and facilitating your loved one's care as well.

Important Documents:

Durable Power of Attorney.

General Power of Attorney

Health Care Power of Attorney

Living Will

Do Not Intubate/Do Not Resuscitate

Will and/or Trust

Advance Directives.

You might consider consulting with an attorney for the following matters:

Care Negligence
Bed Sores
Failure to Monitor
Financial Exploitation
Malnutrition and Dehydration
Home Health Care Directives
Home Medication Errors
Home Physical and sexual Abuse
Slip and Fall Injuries
Wrongful Death Claim

I WON'T BE HERE FOREVER

What support is available when the end is near?

When it comes to talking about the hopes that you or a loved one have for end-of-life care, it's never too early to start the conversation. Although it's not easy to talk about, doing so in advance can help alleviate stress when the time comes to make a choice. Take time to ask yourself or a loved one:

- How and where do I want to live for my remaining days?
- What kind of care do I want?
- Who do I want to provide the care?
- Are there burial plans?

For some, Hospice may be a viable choice. The choice to receive hospice care is always up to the patient (or the designated caregiver, when appropriate). It Iis important to note that the sooner you start hospice care, the sooner you'll be able to take advantage of benefits such as:

- Pain management
- Symptom management
- Life-enriching resources like volunteer visits, music and pet therapy, and legacy planning

Hospice care can start at any time after receiving a terminal illness diagnosis. However, it's most beneficial when there is sufficient time to stabilize your condition and establish a trusting relationship. With proactive symptom management and support 24/7, many hospice patients continue to lead productive and rewarding lives.

Hospice Misconceptions

Hospice Care Is Only for People Who Have Given up on Life

- It is a common misconception that hospice is about dying when, in reality, it is designed to help terminally ill patients

Hospice Care Is Only for People Who Have Given up on Life

- It is a common misconception that hospice is about dying when, in reality, it is designed to help terminally ill patients live their final days to the fullest. It provides medical care and pain management as well as emotional and spiritual support tailored to the patient's needs and desires. The ultimate goal of hospice care is to increase the patient's quality of life and provide support for family members and caretakers to ensure that the patient's final days are as comfortable as possible.

Once You Enter Hospice Care, You Can Never Go Back

- Hospice care is not a death sentence, it is simply a comprehensive service offered to patients with life-limiting illnesses for whom a cure is unlikely or impossible. Patients have the right to leave hospice care at any time. If the patient's condition improves, they may choose to pursue curative treatment again. The option to reapply for hospice always remains open.

- Another common misconception about hospice care is that you must sign a do-not-resuscitate (DNR) order upon entering hospice. A DNR is one of several legal documents patients often choose to include when creating an advanced healthcare directive, but it is by no means a requirement of hospice. The goal of hospice is to provide comfort and support for the patient in whatever form they choose.

Hospice Care Is Only for People with a Few Days or Weeks to Live

- Hospice care is generally intended for patients whose diagnosis limits their life expectancy to no more than 6 months, but individual cases vary.

Entering Hospice Care Means Giving up Control over Your Care

- Hospice care is intended to increase quality of life for terminally ill patients, so it cannot be forced on anyone. This form of care is administered by a team of professionals specially trained to provide care and support to meet the patient's medical, physical, emotional, and spiritual needs, so treatment varies on a case-by-case basis. The patient always has the right to request or refuse services. Hospice patients may even choose to leave hospice and return to curative treatment with the option to return later.

Your Family Has No Control over Your Care Once You Enter Hospice Care

- Hospice care is for the patient's family and loved ones just as much as the patient. Throughout hospice care and following the patient's passing, both the patient and their loved ones have access to support services, including grief counseling, social services, spiritual guidance, and more.

You Need a Doctor's Referral to Enter Hospice Care

- One of the top facts about hospice everyone should know is that anyone can make a referral to hospice. If a family member, friend, or loved one believes a patient could benefit from hospice care, they are allowed to make a referral which will be followed by a doctor's order to qualify the patient for coverage.

Hospice Care Doesn't Make Much of a Difference

- Patients who enter hospice care have already been diagnosed with a terminal illness. Though there may be little to no expectation of a cure, hospice care helps patients live out their remaining days with as little pain, discomfort, and stress as possible.

Hospice Care Ends with the Patient's Passing

- One of the most important hospice myths and facts for families and caregivers to understand is that hospice care does not end with the patient's passing. Bereavement and grief support services are often included for family members for up to a full year after the patient's passing. Many hospice services also help make funeral arrangements or provide support for other issues that arise after the patient's death.

Hospice Care Can Only Be Given at a Hospital or Hospice Facility

- Hospice care can be provided wherever the patient feels most comfortable or wherever services can most effectively be provided. Many patients choose to receive hospice care in the comfort of their own home, though it can also be administered in a hospital, nursing home, assisted living facility, or a hospice center. Hospice is not a location but a method of care focused on pain and symptom management.

Hospice Care and Palliative Care Are the Same Thing

- One of the most important hospice facts any patient should understand is that it is a different service from palliative care. Both palliative care and hospice care alleviate suffering and enhance the quality of life for patients and their loved ones, but hospice care is intended for patients with life-limiting diseases who are no longer pursuing curative treatment. Palliative care can begin as soon as the patient is diagnosed and may be given at the same time as treatment.

Only Patients with Cancer Can Benefit from Hospice Care

- Cancer is universally understood to be one of the most aggressive forms of disease and one of the most difficult to treat. Though this may be true, hospice patients are admitted with a wide variety of diagnoses including heart disease, dementia, lung disease, stroke, and chronic kidney disease.

Hospice Care Is Very Expensive

- Hospice care is a benefit fully funded by Medicare/Medicaid and it is also covered by many private insurance companies.
- Hospice care is also a service covered by the U.S. Department of Veteran's Affairs. Veterans may qualify for hospice care if they meet similar criteria. Most Medicare or Medicaid plans cover hospice care as well as medications, supplies, and medical equipment related to the diagnosis.

COMMON TERMS TO KNOW

Is there help for understanding Healthcare lingo?

Activities of Daily Living (ADLs)

Basic personal activities which include bathing, eating, dressing, mobility, transferring from bed to chair, and using the toilet. ADLs are used to measure how dependent a person may be on requiring assistance in performing any or all of these activities.

Acute Care

Care that is generally provided for a short period of time to treat a certain illness or condition. This type of care can include short-term hospital stays, doctor's visits, surgery, and X-rays. Medical treatment rendered to individuals whose illnesses or health problems are of a short-term or episodic nature. Acute care facilities are those hospitals that mainly serve persons with short-term health problems.

Adult Day Programs

Adult Day programs provide clients with structured activity and, when needed, assistance with activities of daily living (ADLs). There are 2 types of adult day programs: 1) Adult Day Care (ADC), which offers personal care services, and 2) Adult Day Health (ADH), which offers personal care as well as skilled nursing and rehab services. Someday programs are designed specifically for persons needing memory care and support.

Advance Care Planning
The process of discussing, determining and/or executing treatment directives and appointing a proxy decision maker.

Advance Directive for Health Care
(Also called advance directive.) Advance directives are legal documents that allow you to convey your decisions about end-of-life care ahead of time. They provide a way for you to communicate your wishes to family, friends, and health care professionals, and to avoid confusion later on.

- A living will tell how you feel about care intended to sustain life. You can accept or refuse medical care. There are many issues to address, including; The use of dialysis and breathing machines; If you want to be resuscitated if breathing or heartbeat stops; Tube feeding; Organ or tissue donation.

- A durable power of attorney for health care is a document that names your health care proxy. Your proxy is someone you trust to make health decisions if you are unable to do so.

Ancillary Services
Supplemental services, including laboratory, radiology, physical therapy, and inhalation therapy, that are provided in conjunction with medical or hospital care.
Area Agency on Aging (AAA)

A local (city or county) agency, funded under the federal Older Americans Act, that plans and coordinates various social and health service programs for persons 60 years of age or more. The network of AAA offices consists of more than 600 approved agencies.

Assisted Living Communities (ALCs) and Personal Care Homes (PCHs)
ALCs and PCHs provide services to residents who need assistance with personal care, medication management, and/or home management but do not require skilled health care. PCHs range in size from 2 beds in a private home to 100+ apartments. ALCs must have at least 25 apartments. Their services are similar, but eligibility requirements and payment options differ somewhat.

Assistive Devices
Tools that enable individuals with disabilities to perform essential job functions, e.g., telephone headsets, adapted computer keyboards, enhanced computer monitors.

Behavioral Health
An umbrella term that includes mental health and substance abuse, and frequently is used to distinguish from "physical" health. Health care services provided for depression or alcoholism would be considered behavioral health care, while setting a broken leg would be physical health.

Beneficiary
An individual who receives benefits from or is covered by an insurance policy or other health care financing program.

Benefit Start Date of Current Claim Period
The date on which benefit payments began during the reporting period.

Capacity
An individual's ability to understand the significant benefits, risks, and alternatives to proposed health care and to make and communicate a health care decision. The term is frequently used interchangeably with competency but is not the same. Competency is a legal status imposed by the court.

Cardiopulmonary Resuscitation (CPR)
A group of treatments used when someone's heart and/or breathing stops. CPR is used in an attempt to restart the heart and breathing. It usually consists of mouth-to-mouth breathing and pressing on the chest to cause blood to circulate. Electric shock and drugs also are used to restart or control the rhythm of the heart.

Care Plan (also called Service Plan or Treatment Plan)
A Care Plan is a written document which outlines the types and frequency of the long-term care services that a consumer receives. It may include treatment goals for him or her for a specified time period.

Caregiver
Person who provides support and assistance with various activities to a family member, friend, or neighbor. A caregiver may provide emotional or financial support, as well as hands-on help with different tasks. Caregivers can use the formal and informal supports that are available. Caregiving may also be done from long distance.

- An unlicensed assistant who provides direct health related care to patients or residents, a proxy caregiver performing health maintenance activities providing care under the direction and orders of a licensed health care provider.

Care/Case Managers
Offers a single point of entry to the aging services network. Care/case managers assess clients' needs, create service plans, and coordinate and monitor services; they may operate privately or may be employed by social service agencies or public programs. Typically, case managers are nurses or social workers.

Certified Nursing Assistant (I)
A certified nursing assistant has completed required state training and competency testing in the skills required to work as a I.

Chronic Care
Care and treatment given to individuals whose health problems are of a long-term and

continuing nature. Rehabilitation facilities, nursing homes, and mental hospitals may be considered chronic care facilities.

Chronic Disease
A disease that has one or more of the following characteristics: is permanent; leaves residual disability; is caused by nonreversible pathological alternation; requires special training of the patient for rehabilitation; or may be expected to require a long period of supervision, observation, or care.

Chronic Illness
Long-term or permanent illness (e.g., diabetes, arthritis) which often results in some type of disability and which may require a person to seek help with various activities.

Co-Insurance (also called Co-Payment)
The specified portion (dollar amount or percentage) that Medicare, health insurance, or a service program may require a person to pay toward his or her medical bills or services.

- Co-Insurance is a cost-sharing requirement under a health insurance policy. It provides that the insured party will assume a portion or percentage of the costs of covered services. The health insurance policy provides that the insurer will reimburse a specified percentage of all, or certain specified, covered medical expenses in excess of any deductible amounts payable by the insured. The insured is then liable for the remainder of the costs until their maximum liability is reached.

Co-Morbidity
Condition that exists at the same time as the primary condition in the same patient (e.g., hypertension is a co-morbidity of many conditions such as diabetes, ischemic heart disease, end-stage renal disease, etc.).

Co-Payment (also called Co-Insurance)
The specified portion (dollar amount or percentage) that Medicare, health insurance, or a service program may require a person to pay toward his or her medical bills or services.

Cognitive Impairment
Deterioration or loss of intellectual capacity which requires continual supervision to protect the individual or others, as measured by clinical evidence and standardized tests that reliably measure impairment in the area of short or long-term memory, orientation as to person, place, and time, or deductive or abstract reasoning.

Community Care Services Program (CCSP)
A Medicaid waiver program where social workers and registered nurses work as a team to coordinate a range of personal, household, and health-related home and community-based services for clients in their homes.

Continuing Care Retirement Community (CCRC)
CCRCs provide 3 levels of accommodations: independent living, personal care/assisted living, and skilled nursing/rehab. Services vary by level of accommodation. Most CCRCs require new residents to pay a one-time entrance fee prior to admission. Entrance fee refund policies vary. All CCRCs require payment of monthly or daily service fees.

Covered Services
Health care services covered by an insurance plan.

Custodial Care
Care that does not require specialized training or services.

Dementia
Term which describes a group of diseases (including Alzheimer's Disease) which are characterized by memory loss and other declines in mental functioning.

Disability
The limitation of normal physical, mental, social activity of an individual. There are varying types (functional, occupational, learning), degrees (partial, total), and durations (temporary, permanent) of disability. Benefits are often available only for specific disabilities, such as total and permanent (the requirement for Social Security and Medicare).

Discharge
The release of a patient from a provider's care, usually referring to the date at which a patient checks out of a hospital.

Discharge Planner
A discharge planner, often a social worker, is a core member of a hospital patient's care-facilitation team. Working with the attending physician, specialists and bedside nurses, the discharge planner helps to coordinate the patient's transition to life after the hospital, often working with the patient's family, nursing homes, medical-equipment providers, and insurance companies to smoothly facilitate a patient's move to the next level of care.

Do Not Resuscitate Order
(Also called a DNR order, a No CPR order, a DNAR order (do not attempt resuscitation), and an AND order (allow natural death).) [See also Physician Orders for Life-Sustaining Treatment (POLST).] A physician's order written in a patient's medical record indicating that health care providers should not attempt CPR in the event of cardiac or respiratory arrest. In some regions, this order may be transferable between medical venues.

Dual Eligible
A person who is eligible for two health insurance plans, often referring to a Medicare beneficiary who also qualifies for Medicaid benefits.

Durable Medical Equipment (DME)
(Also called Home Medical Equipment) Equipment such as hospital beds, wheelchairs, ventilator, oxygen system, home dialysis system, and prosthetics used at home. DME may be covered by Medicaid and in part by Medicare or private insurance. DME may also be prescribed by a physician for a patient's use for an extended period of time.

Durable Power of Attorney for Health Care
(See Advanced Directive for Health Care) A durable power of attorney for health care is a document that names your health care proxy. Your proxy is someone you trust to make health decisions if you are unable to do so.

Emergency Medical Services (EMS)
Services utilized in responding to the perceived individual need for immediate treatment for medical, physiological, or psychological illness or injury.

Estate Recovery
By law states are required to recover funds from certain deceased Medicaid recipients' estates up to the amount spent by the state for all Medicaid services (e.g., nursing facility, home and community-based services, hospital, and prescription costs).

Family and Medical Leave Act (FMLA)
A 1993 federal law requiring employers with more than 50 employees to provide eligible workers up to 12 weeks of unpaid leave for

birth, adoptions, foster care placement, and illnesses of employees and their families.

Fee-for-Service (FFS)
The way traditional Medicare and health insurance work. Medical providers bill for whatever service they provide. Medicare and/or traditional insurance pay their share, and the patient pays the balance through co-payments and deductibles.

- A payment mechanism in which payment is made for each utilized service. FFS services exclude services provided under capitated arrangements.

Geriatrician
Physician who is certified in the care of older people.

Geriatrics
Medical specialty focusing on treatment of health problems of the elderly.

Gerontology
Study of the biological, psychological, and social processes of aging.

Guardian
A judicially appointed guardian or conservator having authority to make a health care decision for an individual.

Health Insurance
Financial protection against the medical care costs arising from disease or accidental bodily

injury. Such insurance usually covers all or part of the medical costs of treating the disease or injury. Insurance may be obtained on either an individual or a group basis.

Health Insurance Portability and Accountability Act (HIPAA)
Federal health insurance legislation passed in 1996, which sets standards for access, portability, and renewability that apply to group coverage—both fully insured and self-funded—as well as to individual coverage. HIPAA allows under specified conditions, for long-term care insurance policies to be qualified for certain tax benefits under Section 7702(b) of the Internal Revenue Code.

Health Maintenance Organization (HMO)
Managed care organization that offers a range of health services to its members for a set rate, but which requires its members to use health care professionals who are part of its network of providers. (See also Medicare HMOs.)

Home and Community-Based Waivers
Medicaid waiver programs provide supportive services to individuals who are eligible for nursing home placement but want to remain in their homes (private homes, HUD-subsidized communities, non-subsidized retirement communities, personal care homes, assisted living communities, and continuing care retirement communities).

Home and Community Based Services (HCBS)
HCBS organizations provide a range of personal, household, and health-related services to help clients age in place wherever they choose to live. Services are delivered in the client's home (such as home care, home-delivered meals, home hospice, etc.) and/or the organization's own facility/senior center (such as adult day care, adult day health, and congregate meals, etc.). HOME CARE provides one or more of the following categories of services in a client's home: companion/sitting, personal care, and skilled nursing. Home care staff typically spend from 4 to 24 hours in a client's home. However, shorter visits are offered for home care services in some retirement housing communities.

Home Health Care provides short-term, intermittent (not daily) skilled health care services to patients in their homes, typically for up to 60 days, and often following a hospital discharge. Skilled nursing is provided by RNs and LPNs, and rehabilitation services (such as physical therapy and speech therapy) are provided by licensed therapists. A physician's order is required for all services.

Adult Day Programs provide clients with structured activity and, when needed, assistance with activities of daily living (ADLs). There are 2 types of adult day programs: 1) Adult Day Care (ADC), which offers personal care services, and 2) Adult Day Health (ADH), which offers personal care as well as skilled nursing and rehab services. Someday programs are designed specifically for persons needing memory care and support.

Hospice Care provides end-of-life care to patients with a terminal illness and a life expectancy of less than 6 months. Because most people prefer to stay at home, services are usually provided in the home setting as opposed to an in-patient facility. Services are provided by an inter-disciplinary clinical team including nurses, certified nursing assistants (CNAs), social workers, volunteers, bereavement counselors, chaplains, and medical directors.

Respite Care allows family caregivers to have a brief rest by providing temporary, overnight care for the ill or disabled for a few days or weeks.

Home Delivered Meals often called Meals-on-Wheels, bring nutritionally balanced meals to those unable to prepare their own food.

Homebound
One of the requirements to qualify for Medicare home health care. Means that someone is generally unable to leave the house, and if they do leave home, it is only for a short time (e.g., for a medical appointment) and requires much effort.

Homemaker Services
In-home help with meal preparation, shopping, light housekeeping, money management, personal hygiene and grooming, and laundry.

Hospice
Hospice organizations provide end-of-life care to patients with a terminal illness and a life expectancy of less than 6 months. Because most people prefer to stay at home, services are usually provided in the home setting as opposed to an in-patient facility. Services are provided by an inter-disciplinary clinical team including nurses, certified nursing assistants (CNAs), social workers, volunteers, bereavement counselors, chaplains, and medical directors. In-patient hospice care can be delivered in an in-patient hospice facility and in other settings such as a skilled nursing home.

Impairment
Any loss or abnormality of psychological, physiological, or anatomical function.

Independent Living Retirement Communities
All non-subsidized retirement communities offer independent living accommodations. Some also offer personal care/assisted living, and skilled nursing/rehab services. These communities are also known as Senior Living Communities or, in a few cases, Continuing Care Retirement Communities (CCRCs).

Indigent Care
Health services provided to the poor or those unable to pay. Since many indigent patients are not eligible for federal or state programs, the costs which are covered by Medicaid are generally recorded separately from indigent care costs

Inpatient
A person who has been admitted at least overnight to a hospital or other health facility (which is therefore responsible for his or her room and board) for the purpose of receiving diagnostic treatment or other health services.

Level of Care (LOC)
Amount of assistance required by consumers which may determine their eligibility for programs and services. Levels include: protective, intermediate, and skilled.

Life-Sustaining Treatment
Medical procedures that replace or support an essential bodily function. Life-sustaining treatments include CPR, mechanical ventilation, artificial nutrition and hydration, dialysis, and certain other treatments.

Living Will
(See Advanced Directive for Health Care.) A living will tells how you feel about care intended to sustain life. You can accept or refuse medical care. There are many issues to address, including The use of dialysis and breathing machines; If you want to be resuscitated if breathing or heartbeat stops; Tube feeding; Organ or tissue donation.

Long-Term Care (LTC)
Range of medical and/or social services designed to help people who have disabilities or chronic care needs. Services may be short-term or long-term and may be provided in a person's home, in

the community, or in residential facilities (e.g., nursing homes or Assisted Living\Personal Care).

Long-Term Care Insurance (LTCI)
Insurance policies which pay for long-term care services that Medicare and Medigap policies do not cover. Policies vary in terms of what they will cover and may be expensive. Coverage may be denied based on health status or age. Consumers who qualify can pay out of pocket for long-term care insurance. Benefits vary widely among policies, but most have some type of coverage for long-term nursing home care, home care, personal care/assisted living, adult day care, and adult day health.

Long-Term Care Ombudsman
An individual designated by a state or a substate unit responsible for investigating and resolving complaints made by or for older people in long-term care facilities. Also responsible for monitoring federal and state policies that relate to long-term care facilities, for providing information to the public about the problems of older people in facilities, and for training volunteers to help in the ombudsman program. The long-term care ombudsman program is authorized by Title III of the Older Americans Act.

Managed Care (MC)
Method of organizing and financing health care services which emphasizes cost-effectiveness and coordination of care. Managed care

organizations (including HMOs, PPOs, and PSOs) receive a fixed amount of money per client/member per month (called a capitation), no matter how much care a member needs during that month.

- Payment mechanism used to manage health care, including services provided by health maintenance organizations or Programs of All-Inclusive Care for the Elderly, prepaid health plans, and primary care case management plans.

Medicaid Waiver Programs
Medicaid waiver programs provide supportive services to individuals who are eligible for nursing home placement but want to remain in their homes (private homes, HUD communities, retirement communities, personal care homes, assisted living communities, and continuing care retirement communities).

Medical Necessity
Services or supplies which are appropriate and consistent with the diagnosis in accord with accepted standards of community practice and are not considered experimental. They also cannot be omitted without adversely affecting the individual's condition or the quality of medical care.

Medically Indigent
People who cannot afford needed health care because of insufficient income and/or lack of adequate health insurance.

Medicare (Title XVIII)
Medicare is a federal health insurance program for persons over the age of 65. There are 4 categories of coverage:
Medicare Part A: Pays toward hospital room and board, home health care, skilled nursing home care and rehab in a skilled nursing home, and hospice care.
Medicare Part B: Pays toward doctors' fees and other outpatient services.
Medicare Part C: Allows people to choose a Medicare Advantage Plan, thus opting out of traditional Medicare Parts A and B.
Medicare Part D: Pays toward prescription drug coverage.

Medicare HMOs
Under Medicare HMOs (health maintenance organizations), members pay their regular monthly premiums to Medicare, while Medicare pays the HMO a fixed sum of money each month to provide Medicare benefits (e.g., hospitalization, doctor's visits, and more). Medicare HMOs may provide extra benefits over and above regular Medicare benefits (such as prescription drug coverage, eyeglasses, and more). Members do not pay Medicare deductibles and co-payments; however, the HMO may require them to pay an additional monthly premium and co-payments for some

services. If members use providers outside the HMO's network, they pay the entire bill themselves unless the plan has a point of service option.

Medicare Supplement Insurance (Med SUPP)
(Also called Medigap.) Insurance supplement to Medicare that is designed to fill in the "gaps" left by Medicare (such as co-payments). May pay for some limited long-term care expenses, depending on the benefits package purchased.

Mental Health
The capacity in an individual to function effectively in society. Mental health is a concept influenced by biological, environmental, emotional, and cultural factors and is highly variable in definition, depending on time and place. It is often defined in practice as the absence of any identifiable or significant mental disorder and sometimes improperly used as a synonym for mental illness.

Mental Illness/Impairment
A deficiency in the ability to think, perceive, reason, or remember, which results in loss of the ability to take care of one's daily living needs.
Money Follows the Person (MFP)
Money Follows the Person (MFP) is a rebalancing initiative that was made possible by an eleven-year grant to states from the Centers for Medicare and Medicaid Services (CMS). This grant is designed to help individuals who are institutionalized in nursing facilities and intermediate care facilities (ICF) for people with

developmental disabilities return to their homes and communities.

Morbidity
The extent of illness, injury, or disability in a defined population. It is usually expressed in general or specific rates of incidence or prevalence.

Mortality
Death. Used to describe the relation of deaths to the population in which they occur.

Nonprofit/Not-For-Profit
An organization that reinvests all profits back into that organization.

Nurse
An individual trained to care for the sick, aged, or injured. Can be defined as a professional qualified by education and authorized by law to practice nursing.

Nurse Practitioner (NP)
A registered nurse working in an expanded nursing role, usually with a focus on meeting primary health care needs. NPs conduct physical examinations, interpret laboratory results, select plans of treatment, identify medication requirements, and perform certain medical management activities for selected health conditions. Some NPs specialize in geriatric care.

Occupational Therapy (OT)
Designed to help patients improve their independence with activities of daily living through rehabilitation, exercises, and the use of assistive devices. Occupational Therapy may be covered in part by Medicare.

Ombudsman
A representative of a public agency or a private nonprofit organization who investigates and resolves complaints made by or on behalf of older individuals who are residents of long-term care facilities.

Outpatient
A patient who is receiving ambulatory care at a hospital or other facility without being admitted to the facility. Usually, it does not mean people receiving services from a physician's office or other program which also does not provide inpatient care.

Palliative Care (also called Comfort Care)
A comprehensive approach to treating serious illness that focuses on the physical, psychological, and spiritual needs of the patient. Its goal is to achieve the best quality of life available to the patient by relieving suffering, controlling pain and symptoms, and enabling the patient to achieve maximum functional capacity. Respect for the patient's culture, beliefs, and values is an essential component.

Permanent Vegetative State (PVS)

A vegetative state is a clinical condition of complete unawareness of the self and the environment accompanied by sleep-wake cycles with either complete or partial preservation of hypothalamic and brainstem autonomic functions. The PVS is a vegetative state present at one month after acute traumatic or non-traumatic brain injury, and present for at least one month in degenerative/metabolic disorders or developmental malformations. A PVS can be diagnosed on clinical grounds with a high degree of medical certainty in most adult and pediatric patients after careful, repeated neurologic examinations by a physician competent in neurologic function assessment and diagnosis. A PVS patient becomes permanently vegetative when the diagnosis of irreversibility can be established with a high degree of clinical certainty (i.e., when the chance of regaining consciousness is exceedingly rare).

Personal Care Homes (PCHs) and Assisted Living Communities (ALCs)

PCHs and ALCs provide services to residents who need assistance with personal care, medication management, and/or home management but do not require skilled health care. PCHs range in size from 2 beds in a private home to 100+ apartments. ALCs must have at least 25 apartments. Their services are similar, but eligibility requirements and payment options differ somewhat.

Physical Therapy (PT)
Designed to restore/improve movement and strength in people whose mobility has been impaired by injury and disease. May include exercise, massage, water therapy, and assistive devices. May be covered in part by Medicare.

Qualifying Condition
The specific conditions for which the individual qualifies as chronically ill. This could include dependency in the required number of ADLs, cognitive impairment or both.

Quality of Care
Quality of Care can be defined as a measure of the degree to which delivered health services meet established professional standards and judgments of value to the consumer.

Registered Nurse (RN)
A nurse who has graduated from a formal program of nursing education and has been licensed by an appropriate state authority. RNs are the most highly educated of nurses with the widest scope of responsibility, including all aspects of nursing care. RNs can be graduated from one of three educational programs: two-year associate degree program, three-year hospital diploma program, or four-year baccalaureate program.

Rehabilitation
The combined and coordinated use of medical, social, educational, and vocational measures for training or retaining individuals disabled by

disease or injury to the highest possible level of functional ability. Several different types of rehabilitation are distinguished: vocational, social, psychological, medical, and educational.

Rehabilitation Services
Services designed to improve/restore a person's functioning; includes physical therapy, occupational therapy, and/or speech therapy. Rehabilitation Services may be provided at home or in long-term care facilities and may be covered in part by Medicare.

Reimbursement
The process by which health care providers receive payment for their services. Because of the nature of the health care environment, providers are often reimbursed by third parties who insure and represent patients.
Respiratory Therapy
The diagnostic evaluation, management, and treatment of the care of patients with deficiencies and abnormalities in the cardiopulmonary (heart-lung) system.

Respite Care
Service in which trained professionals or volunteers come into the home to provide short-term care (from a few hours to a few days) for an older person to allow caregivers some time away from their caregiving role.

Retirement Communities (Non-Subsidized)
All non-subsidized retirement communities offer independent living accommodations. Some also

offer personal care/assisted living and skilled nursing/rehab services. These communities are also known as Senior Living Communities, Independent Living Retirement Communities or, in a few cases, Continuing Care Retirement Communities (CCRCs).

Senior Living Communities

All non-subsidized retirement communities offer independent living accommodations for seniors. Some also offer personal care/assisted living and skilled nursing/rehab services. These communities are also known as Independent Living Retirement Communities or, in a few cases, Continuing Care Retirement Communities (CCRCs).

Senior Center

Provides a variety of on-site programs for older adults including recreation, socialization, congregate meals, and some health services. Senior centers are usually a good source of information about area programs and services.

Service Plan (also called Care Plan or Treatment Plan)

A Service Plan is a written document which outlines the types and frequency of the long-term care services that a consumer receives. It may include treatment goals for him or her for a specified time period.

Severity of Illness

A risk prediction system to correlate the "seriousness" of a disease in a particular patient with the statistically "expected" outcome (e.g., mortality, morbidity, efficiency of care).

Skilled Care
"Higher level" of care (such as injections, catheterizations, and dressing changes) provided by trained medical professionals, including nurses, doctors, and physical therapist.

Skilled Nursing Care
Daily nursing and rehabilitative care, prescribed by a physician, that can be performed only by or under the supervision of skilled medical personnel.

Skilled Nursing Facility (SNF)
Skilled Nursing Facilities (also called Skilled Nursing Homes/Rehab) offer two levels of care: long-term care and short-term rehab. Upon discharge from rehab, patients often need follow-up care in their homes. Prior to discharge, nursing home staff coordinate home- and community-based services delivered in the patient's home, such as home health care, home care, medical equipment, etc.

Skilled Nursing Homes/Rehab
Skilled Nursing Homes/Rehab (also called Skilled Nursing Facilities) offer two levels of care: long-term care and short-term rehab. Upon discharge from rehab, patients often need follow-up care in their homes. Prior to discharge, nursing home staff coordinate home- and community-based services delivered in the

patient's home, such as home health care, home care, medical equipment, etc.

Social Security Disability Insurance (SSDI)
A system of federally provided payments to eligible workers (and, in some cases, their families) when they are unable to continue working because of a disability. Benefits begin with the sixth full month of disability and continue until the individual is capable of substantial gainful activity.

Speech Therapy
Designed to help restore speech through exercises. Speech Therapy may be covered by Medicare.

Spend-Down
Medicaid financial eligibility requirements are strict and may require beneficiaries to spend down/use up assets or income until they reach the eligibility level.

Supplemental Security Income (SSI)
A program of support for low-income aged, blind, and disabled persons, established by Title XVI of the Social Security Act.

Support Groups
Groups of people who share a common bond (e.g., caregivers) who come together on a regular basis to share problems and experiences. Support Groups may be sponsored by social service agencies, senior centers, religious

organizations, as well as organizations such as the Alzheimer's Association.

Surrogate
(Also called proxy by default.) A Surrogate is a person who, by default, becomes the proxy decision maker for an individual who has no appointed agent.

Veterans' Aid and Attendance (A & A)
Aid and Attendance is a benefit paid by Veterans Affairs to a veteran, veteran's spouse, or surviving spouse needing home care, personal care/assisted living, or long-term nursing home care. There are income and asset limitations for eligibility. There are other benefits programs for veterans in addition to Aid and Attendance. Go to the Veterans Administration website for additional information.

Veterans' Disability Compensation Program
An individual must have a partial or total impairment by injury or disease incurred or aggravated during military service. A Veterans' Affairs (VA) rating board employs criteria developed by the VA to rate the extent of a disability.

Veterans' Disability Pension Program
An individual must have an injury or disease sustained outside of military service regarding a veteran permanently and totally impaired. Impairment is determined based on the veteran's ability to function at work and at home.

Veterans' Health Services Programs
Veterans' Affairs (VA) hospitals are required to provide care to Class A veterans defined as those: rated as "service-connected; retired from active duty for a disability incurred or aggravated while in military service; in receipt of a VA pension; eligible for Medicaid; a former POW; in need of care for a condition that is possibly related to exposure to dioxin or other toxic substance; in need of care for a condition possibly related to exposure to radiation from nuclear tests or in the American occupation of Japan; or has an income below $16,466 with no dependents; or $19,759 with one dependent (with $1,055 added for each additional dependent). VA hospitals provide care on a space-available basis to persons in Category B veterans, those whose disabilities are not service-connected and have incomes above $16,466 but below $21,954. (Category C veterans have higher incomes and must pay a copayment.)

Withholding/Withdrawing Treatment
Forgoing or discontinuing life-sustaining measures.

REFERENCES

Helping Family and Friends. Alzheimer's Disease and Dementia. (n.d.). https://www.alz.org/help-support/i-have-alz/live-well/helping-family-friends.

Home. Home - ClinicalTrials.gov. (n.d.). https://clinicaltrials.gov/.

https://www.agingcare.com/articles/how-to-create-a-care-plan-195526.htm Elderly Patients in Hospital. (n.d.).

Mayo Foundation for Medical Education and Research. (2019, April 19). *Dementia.* Mayo Clinic. https://www.mayoclinic.org/diseases-conditions/dementia/symptoms-causes/syc-20352013.

Mayo Foundation for Medical Education and Research. (2020, November 19). *Aging: What to expect*. Mayo Clinic. https://www.mayoclinic.org/healthy-lifestyle/healthy-aging/in-depth/aging/art-20046070.

Senior Housing Payment Options. Senior Housing | Senior Living | Senior Apartments. (2020, May 27). https://www.seniorhousingnet.com/advice-and-planning/senior-housing-payment-options.

U.S. Department of Health and Human Services. (n.d.). *What Is Dementia? Symptoms, Types, and Diagnosis*. National Institute on Aging. https://www.nia.nih.gov/health/what-dementia-symptoms-types-and-diagnosis.

What's New! Center for Positive Aging Atlanta, Georgia - Home. (n.d.). http://www.centerforpositiveaging.org/.

Things to Know.

Name: ____________________ DOB: ____________________________ SS# ________________________

Address: _____________________________________ Phone: _________________________

____ Email: _________________________

____

Primary Care Physician: ________________________________ Phone: ____________________________

Specialist: ____ Phone: ____________________________

Specialist: ____ Phone: ____________________________

Specialist: ____ Phone: ____________________________

Diagnosis: ____ Medication: _______________________

Diagnosis: ____ Medication: _______________________

Diagnosis: ____ Medication: _______________________

Diagnosis: ____ Medication: _______________________

Diagnosis: ____ Medication: _______________________

Allergies: ____

Limitations: ____

____

Emergency Contact: ___________________________________ Phone: ___________________________

Healthcare Power of Attorney: __________________________ Phone: ___________________________

Financial Power of Attorney: ____________________________ Phone: ___________________________

Health Insurance Provider: ______________________________ Phone: ___________________________

Member ID# ____________________________________ Group# ___________________________

Health Insurance Provider: ______________________________ Phone: ___________________________

Member ID# ____________________________________ Phone: ___________________________

Life Insurance Provider: ________________________________ Phone# ___________________________

Policy # ____________________________________

Life Insurance Provider: ________________________________ Phone# ___________________________

Policy# ____________________________________

Notes: ____

____

____

____

ABOUT THE AUTHOR

Dr. Mondresia Carver is the Founder & CEO of My Peace of Mind (MyPOM), a senior service company that has been designed to assist seniors and their families in attaining their maximum quality of life throughout the aging process. Dr. Mondresia understands the need for extensive knowledge about costs, quality, and availability of community resources. MyPOM offers the expert guidance in several fields to include social work, psychology, and nursing with specialized focus on issues related to aging and elder care.

She has extensive professional experience working with the senior population. Dr. Mondresia offers a wealth of information from multiple aspects of the aging process. As a General Manager for an Assisted Living community, Director of Social Services for multiple skilled nursing facilities, Mental Health therapist, Care Manager, Hospice/Home Health and Placement consultant, she has become a strong advocate for seniors and their families. She has also been able to use her skills and knowledge to bridge the physiological, psychological, and sociological aspects of the aging process.

Dr. Mondresia has always had a notable affection and rapport with the elderly, having a very close relationship with her own grandparents. She is aware that as our loved ones age, we want to be there for them as much as we can. Our ultimate desire is to respect their wish to remain as independent as possible. However, circumstances may prevent that from being a reality. During those times, Dr. Mondresia understands the anxiety and fear that the unknown may cause.

Caring for the elderly presents several significant challenges, especially patients with impaired communication or cognitive status deficits. There is a special place in Dr. Mondresia's heart to assure that this unique population receives the care that they both need and deserve.

www.ingramcontent.com/pod-product-compliance
Lightning Source LLC
LaVergne TN
LVHW020658100826
845148LV00012B/2547

* 9 7 8 1 7 3 6 3 0 3 2 9 0 *